THOM PAIN
(based on nothing)

THOM PAIN
(based on nothing)

published with other
monologues for theatre

Will Eno

THEATRE COMMUNICATIONS GROUP
NEW YORK
2018

Thom Pain (based on nothing) is published by Theatre Communications Group, Inc., 520 Eighth Avenue, 24th Floor, New York, NY 10018-4156

Thom Pain (based on nothing) is published by arrangement with Oberon Books, Ltd. 521 Caledonia Road, London, N7 9RH

"Mr Theatre Comes Home Different" originally appeared in *Post Road*, Vol. 4, and appears here with gratitude to the editors.

The publication of *Thom Pain (based on nothing)* by Will Eno, through TCG's Book Program, is made possible in part by the New York State Council on the Arts with support of Governor Andrew Cuomo and the New York State Legislature.

TCG books are exclusively distributed to the book trade by Consortium Book Sales and Distribution.

A catalogue record for this book is available from the Library of Congress

ISBN 978-1- 55936-959-6 (trade paper)
ISBN 978-1-55936-922-0 (ebook)

Cover image: Michael C. Hall from *Thom Pain*, photo by Tristan Nash/ Signature Theatre

First TCG Edition, March 2005
Revised TCG Edition, November 2018

THANK YOU and LOVE,
MARIA, ALBERTINE, MADELEINE,
JOHN, GORDON, and JIM.

Contents

THOM PAIN

(based on nothing)

DRAMATIS PERSONAE

THOM PAIN

Male, 30s-40s, cold, grave, somewhat angular person. A wounded, stray-dog type, but with an odd intellectual aspect, perhaps even a little frail, in some way. He should seem capable of great cruelty, perhaps due to his having suffered great cruelties, himself. He must also be charismatic, must be able to 'run the show,' but run it without a lot of effort, relying more on a kind of dark seductive quality. He is somewhere between Shakespeare's Richard II and his Richard III. That said, the actor must also create a character that is close to – and is largely derived from – himself.

AUDIENCE

Female, male, various ages.

Setting: *A mostly empty stage, the theatre.*

Wardrobe: *Plain dark suit, white shirt, dark tie. Clothes should be non-descript: slightly-worn, not of a perfect fit, though certainly not ragged.*

A props list and some general notes are at the end of the play.

Thom Pain was first produced by Soho Theatre Company in association with Chantal Arts + Theatre and Naked Angels (NYC) at the Pleasance Courtyard, Edinburgh on 5 August 2004, before transferring to Soho Theatre, London on 3 September. The personnel were:

THOM PAIN, James Urbaniak

Director, Hal Brooks
Artistic Associate, Julie Anderson
Design Consultant, David Korins
Lighting Designer, Christoph Wagner

On its transfer to DR2 Theatre, New York, on 1 February 2005, *Thom Pain* was produced by Daryl Roth and Bob Boyett with the following personnel:

THOM PAIN, James Urbaniak

Director, Hal Brooks
Artistic Associate, Julie Anderson
Design Consultant, David Korins
Lighting Designer, Mark Barton
General Manager, Adam Hess

Thom Pain (based on nothing) opened on November 11, 2018 at Signature Theatre (Paige Evans, Artistic Director; Harold Wolpert, Executive Director; Jim Houghton, Founder) in New York City. It was directed by Oliver Butler, the set design was by Amy Rubin, the costume design was by Anita Yavich, the lighting design was by Jen Schriever, the sound design was by Lee Kinney; the production stage manager was Charles M. Turner III, the production assistant was Elizabeth Emanuel, and the assistant director was Banna Desta.

The cast was:

THOM PAIN, Michael C. Hall

THOM PAIN

Enters in darkness. Footsteps are heard. A match is lit, to light a cigarette. It is snuffed out, accidentally, without the cigarette being lit. The darkness remains.

How wonderful to see you all.

A second match is lit, and is, again, accidentally snuffed out.

I should quit.

Pause. It's still dark.

We should define some terms here. Then, maybe, you get a little story. So. From the New Century Dictionary of English *(Rustling of paper, in the dark.)*:

Quote, "Fear:

1. Any of the discrete parts of the face, as in the eyes or mouth, or eyes.

2. The capital of Lower Meersham, in the north central southeast corner. Population 8,000,001, approx.

3. Fear.

4. See three.

5. There is no seven.

Colloquial. Archaic. A verb. Or noun. Depends." End quote.

(Rustling of pages. The following lines are said somewhat to himself.) Hey, look at that. "Felicific. Adjective. Causing or intending to cause happiness." *(Very softly.)* Felicific.

Anyway. Now. I guess we begin. Do you like magic? I don't. Enough about me. Let's get to our story. Do you want a story? Do you need to see me to hear me? If so, sorry. Not yet. I'm afraid you'd laugh at my native costume. Promise you won't laugh. I know you won't, friends, I trust you won't. But not because you promised. You'll see me soon enough, I suspect. But not yet.

For now, we should take a moment to consider –

A flash of bright light lights up the whole stage, and then, more-focused light comes up on THOM PAIN. This light cue should only take a split-second: a flash and then lights up. It should have a jarring and accidental feel. THOM is caught off-center, though he quickly adjusts.

And yet. I guess some things are not really ours to decide. The shape of the face, say, or whether we're forgiven or how tall we are. Where to die and when.

Brief pause.

I'll wait for the laughter to die down.

Brief pause.

I still sense some laughter.

Brief pause.

There. Wait. Now. There.

Brief pause.

Oh, me.

So. Our story. Don't make it hard on yourselves. Don't be troubled by what you might perceive as obscure, hard, troublous. Just remember the simple human picture before you. This.

Brief pause.

A little boy in a cowboy suit, writing in a puddle with a stick, a dog approaching. Deaf or dumb, the boy is, or, like anyone, a little timid, partly stupid, ashamed, afraid, like us, like you. Our little boy is wearing shorts, shoes, no socks, no cowboy boots. He is there. Dreaming of this real life right here. Picture the boy. A terrible storm has just ended. A cloud, overhead, a little rumble. The boy writes his watery lines. See his eyes. Sympathize with his little clothes. Now, break his arm, give him an injury, some problem with his hip so that he stands funny, can't walk "real good." Now picture that the stick he is writing with is a violin bow. Picture a violin section. Picture every living person as a member of a violin section. We hold the bow above the strings, ready to play. Picture a bird settling on a branch. The violins are on fire. Feel the world inhale. Picture the readiness, the stillness, the virtuosity. Among this, the child. Picture ash blowing across a newly-blue sky. *(The following is said almost without anger, as if it's just another request, as in "Picture a violin section.")* Now go fuck yourselves.

He takes out a small box of raisins and eats some, staring at the audience.

Picture, I don't know, a bird. Or the kid, the child. Picture whatever you want. You're free, at least to this little extent, yes? Who knows. Not me.

Brief pause.

You know who I suddenly don't need?

Very brief pause.

Anyone?

No, I don't know, either. No bother. Or – to employ the popular phrase we use today to express our brainless and simpering tolerance of everything, the breakdown of distinction, our fading national soul – whatever.

Casually.

I'm like whatever.

Pointedly. As if a grave admission.

I really am like whatever.

THOM moves downstage.

Does it scare you? Being face to face with the modern mind? It should. There is no reason for you not to be afraid. None. Or, I don't know. *(Gently.)* Shall I save your life? Shall I love you slowly and be true? Shall I stroke your cheek, gently, almost not at all, and bring you a glass of cold water in the restless humid night? Whatever.

Pause. He returns upstage, turning his back for a moment. As he begins the following lines, a man in the audience, seated in the fourth or fifth row, begins to leave. The man is not angry or offended, and leaves quickly and quietly. It is as if he has suddenly realized that he is in the wrong show and is meant to be at the theatre down the street. THOM notices him but tries to ignore him.

Meanwhile, we were speaking of the infant, the cowboy-suited child, making his way in the business world. A tale for the ages, a flowery unfolding that will leave you yearning for that old yearning that –

(To the man who is leaving.) Goodbye.

The man is gone. Quietly:

Au revoir, cunt. Pardon my French.

THOM starts to return to a story-telling mode. Then, something occurs to him to say, with reference to the man who left.

I'm like him. I strike people as a person who just left.

But, our little performance, our little turn, on the themes of fear, boyhood, nature, hate, the nature of performance and vice-versa, the heart of man, of woman, et cetera.

You know, you might be better off if you had gone with your
heart and left, like our friend, now departed, who just left
with his heart. And the rest of his organs. I don't know. This
was an aside. Pretend I didn't say it. Don't imagine a pink
elephant.

Brief pause.

Yes, our little story, the little boy in the cowboy suit. Did I
say he had a cowboy suit? Not important. Did I say he had
a heart and body full of bleeding wonder and love? Not
important. Either way, there is our little man, before the
puddle, in the quiet after the storm. There is a little thunder
but no more rain. Not unimportantly, the sky is all blue now.
Blue skies for Child Harold, whose name is not Harold. Trees
are down, branches everywhere. The boy's beloved dog
jogs toward him, daintily avoiding other yet-to-be-written-in
puddles. She's been making her rounds, pawing around the
bases of trees and sniffing butterflies drying themselves in the
breeze. Ah, the dog. Long story short, boy loves dog, dog
loves boy, no question, no amendment, no need to revise.
The dog came closer, stopped to scratch. *(Without pausing,
he becomes distracted by some lint on the sleeve of his jacket or
somewhere on his clothes and removes it, as he speaks the next two
lines.)* Then she lowered her head to lap water from a puddle
and was electrocuted. A power line had come down and was
lying frayed in the water. She was thrown some distance, flew
like some poorly thought-out bird. Her eyes were burned
open and smoking; the pads on her paws had blistered off.
She was dead instantly, veterinarians and electrical engineers
would later agree. Poor dog. The boy laughed and laughed
and wrote maniacally into his puddle. We don't know why.
Trust me, that this happened, and happened, like this. He
went over to her, knelt down by her. He opened the jaws
and tried to put his ear in the mouth. The dog had white
markings above her paws. He patted it. Oh, the clear blue
sky, the whitish backs of the leaves in the breeze, the feeling

of the world, renewed but still the same. The boy yawned. A car came by, slowed, passed. An everyday moment. The boy swallowed. He lived through this.

Questions? *(Brief pause.)* No?

I have one.

When did *your* childhood end? How badly did *you* get hurt, when you did, when you were this little, when you were this wee little hurtable thing, nothing but big eyes, a heart, a few hundred words? Isn't it wonderful how we never recover? Injuries and wounds, ladies and gents. Slights and abuses, oh, what a paradise. Living in fear, suiting the hurt to our need. I'm serious. What a happy life. What a good game. Who can stand the most, the most life, and still smile, still grin into the coming night saying more, more, encore, encore, you fuckers, you gods, just give me more of the bloody bloody same. *(Brief pause.)* Or, I don't know, what do I know?

People ask about the name. "Thom Pain." I don't answer. Or I say, "It's been in the family a while." Or I say, "Child Harold," for no reason. Then one of us walks away.

Anyway, the boy lay down behind the dog, holding her. He closed his own eyes with his fingers. The boy lay in a puddle behind his former dog, whispering, "I do. I do." He came home later, without stick or dog. No one noticed him, the change in him. The boy got some scissors and cut his hair half-off. He drew a simple bone on his stomach with some of his mother's lipstick. He tucked himself badly into bed. He sang a little song without words or tune. He lay there, awake, breathing too much, biting a crayon, trying to hold everything in. The boy smelled of dead wet dog. His legs shook and he wet his bed. *(Brief pause.)* This all being an example of – I don't know – how some days can go, of actual life, of the close relations between man and animal.

Now, imagine a pink elephant. Now, stop.

Brief pause.

Good. Wait a minute? There. Thank you, sir.

Pause.

(With earnest enthusiasm.) Now I think would be a good time for the raffle. I hope you held on to your tickets, on the back of which is a number. We have some very nice prizes.

He moves off the stage, perhaps to a back area, checking his pockets, looking back to the lighting booth, etc.

All right, are you ready? Okay. Here we go. Who's feeling lucky, who's got the luck? This'll be fun.

Brief pause.

There is no raffle. Who said there was going to be a raffle? The good news is, you didn't lose. You lost nothing except the time it took to find this out. Which is a pretty big chunk. Someday, some minute, you'll have thirty seconds to live. Think of me, my little comic bit about the raffle. Think of me, fucking around with your life, and try to smile.

Trust me, there are people out there who don't love you. Who don't love you enough to spit on your little hopes, so as to leave you all alone, respectfully and truly alone, with your larger ones. Your larger hopes. Which are what? *(To a man in the audience.)* Sir? Care to share your larger hopes with us? *(After a brief pause.)* No? That's fine. I understand. Don't want to jinx anything. Or have nothing to jinx. Or can't feel hope. Or don't like sharing. Oh, the varieties of experience. Feel free to feel anything. Religious ecstasy, Anarchy, Shivery physical things, Nothing, Blood, Your neighbor, That stranger you married. What possibilities we all have here, ways and means to live and die. Cancer, for example, or depression. Anxiety, Insecurity, Holes in your knowledge, Spots on your lungs, Total oblivion. Sky-diving. *(Brief pause.)* Financial crisis, Outer space, Inner peace, Shame, Lust, Heavy-heartedness, Light-headedness, Sympathy, God, a Migraine, Me, Words, Sounds, Afraid, the Past, Present...God. The things you may be feeling. The list goes on. Then the list ends.

(The next two lines or so are directed toward a specific person somewhere in the first row.) If I were you, I'd be sick of this already. I'd feel restless. I'd feel like eating or urinating. I think that covers it. Or maybe I'd feel like taking a long walk on a long pier. Or I'd feel sorry. For me. If I were you. I don't know, really. But, again, feel whatever you like. As if you need me to tell you that. It's your life. Yes?

(To a particular person in the audience.) What if you only had one day to live? What would you do? That's easy. You'd be brave and true and reckless. You would love life and people with wild and new abandon. If you only had a day. *(Very brief pause.)* What if you only had forty years? What would you do? If you're like me, and – no offense, but – you probably are, you wouldn't do anything. It's sad, isn't it? This dead horse of a life we beat, all the wilder, all the harder the deader it gets. On the other hand, there are some nice shops in the area. I bought a candle-holder and a chair, today. I lost the candle-holder somewhere.

Pause. The following is announced exactly the same as when announced before.

Now I think would be a good time for the raffle. I hope you held on to your tick– no. Sorry, where was I? I was thinking about your life. Very distracting. Okay. *(Lines spoken quickly, as he seeks to find his place again.)* I bought a candle-holder and a chair today. I lost the candle-holder somewhere. Okay. Sorry. I bought a – Huh.

Brief pause.

Well, while we're waiting. So, a horse walks into a bar. The bartender says, "Why the long face?" And the horse says, "I'm dying of AIDS. And I guess I feel a little sorry for myself." So the bartender says, "My God, that's awful. I'm so sorry."

Brief pause.

I'm forgetting some part of it. But you get the point, you see the hilarity. It's funny because it's true.

Brief pause.

What a nice crowd. I see no difference, really. In a world filled with difference, sickening disheartening difference, I see none. Between the you and the me. You all seem so wonderful and I seem so wonderful, and so I make no distinction, I see no separation, no unbridgeable distance between us, wonderful us. Or none worth remarking, since the thought of you disgusts me so much. The thought of you doesn't disgust me that much. In fact, you're all so wonderful, I'd like to take you home, leave you there, and then go somewhere else. No, seriously. The truth? I don't care either way. That's not true. I do care, either way.

I'm the type of person you might not hear from for sometime, but then, suddenly, one day, bang, you never hear from me again.

We're all roughly this way, yeah? Roughly.

Noting a woman in the audience.

Except you. You're different. I really love your difference, it's so wonderful and lovely and different. *(He moves closer to her, perhaps kneeling or stepping off-stage.)* Where are you from, I wonder, or, did wonder, about two seconds ago. *(He retreats.)* But now that's over, we're through. Sorry. See you around. You can throw my things away. I would change the locks if I were you. *(Solemnly.)* Bye now.

23

Reality is funny, sometimes. Not to me.

Let's talk a little about love.

Brief pause. Perhaps looking at the woman to whom he was just speaking, as if waiting for her to begin the conversation.

I see. Fine. I'll begin. Do you like magic? I do. It's fairly new, this love of mine, of magic. I made serious inroads into a woman, once, doing card tricks with a deck that only had one card left in it. "Pick a card," I'd say. She would lick her lips, touch herself or me, maybe we'd laugh, maybe not. She wasn't from here. So I had to speak to her in the international language of love: English. But we had some laughs – two. No, three. We had an understanding, though neither of us knew what it was. But we were pretty compatible, for a while there, what with our – the different sexual organs. Anyway, here we are together – eating, sleeping, holding each other. The jargon of romance is almost unbearably precise: Going steady, Seeing each other, Going out. It takes a serious dose of shaking, vision loss, and a year of staying in, to understand the beauty of those terms, the pain and wonder in the words. Anyway, this was us, a couple, partners, un-apart. Whispers like you've never heard.

"You've changed," she said, the night we met. She had watchful eyes, sober sometimes, a natural sort of animal guardedness I thought I recognized. Sometimes you meet someone who you know right away is made up of trillions of different cells, and, she was one of these. A quivering thing, a good vocabulary, nice legs, pretty eyes, the backside. Apologies for the dirty language. But it's all dirty language, if you look at it right.

As for our story, if you're lost at all, you're not alone. Don't think I'm somewhere out ahead, somewhere anywhere, with a plan. I'm right here beside you, or hiding behind you, like you, in terrible pain, trying to make sense of my life. I'm just kidding – you probably are alone. Or, I don't know. Where are we, exactly, I wonder, in your estimation, in mine.

Earth is always an answer.

We're on planet Earth, a planet in a solar system, one of a trillion solar systems in our galaxy, which is one of a billion galaxies in the Universe. And you think you're pretty special. Math. There's a lot of zeroes out there. What can one man do? Nothing, really. Or I don't know. I've been taking vitamin supplements. A – no, yeah – A. B. D. Zinc. Actually, zinc is a mineral. You don't care. C. E. Did I say B? I don't care.

Do me a favor. If you have a home, when you're home, later, avoiding your family, staring at the dog, and they ask you where you've been, please just don't say that you were out somewhere watching someone being clever, watching some smart-mouthed nobody work himself into some dumb-ass frenzy. Please say instead, when you don't say anything because no one asked you, that you saw someone who was trying. I choose the word with care. I'm trying. A trying man. A feeling thing, in a wordy body. Poor Thom's a-trying. Poor Thom is fucking cold. I imagine you people have some experience with the Elizabethans. Or some experience with cold. Or maybe a memorable splinter?

Anyway.

So, the child – no, the woman. Let me linger with my woman a little longer. She still had her tonsils, her appendix, her wisdom teeth, all the beautiful useless extra things. This, plus the holes, the holes in her body, in her childhood, the missing things, the blind spots. Altogether, with the pluses and the minuses, a very complete woman. *(Brief pause.)* I loved her so much. So beautiful, my God. She had – *(He moves to one side of the stage, perhaps in front of a curtain, into darkness – perhaps seeking a quiet private place from which to speak great intimate truths. Speaks as if to the stage manager in the booth.)* Could I have a little light over here? *(He waits. No light comes up. He returns to exactly where he stood before, and begins again, exactly as before.)* I loved her so much. So beautiful, my God. She had everything. She had fleas, which I think I gave her, and, moles and birthmarks that she came up with on her own. A healthy give and take. We were very close. She felt, wrongly, that she could tell me anything. I think of her in the evenings. Should I hear a plangent honking and raise my eyes to descry in the darkening sky a vee of geese, heading north or south, I take my pulse and remember those –

To the woman in the audience to whom THOM spoke, earlier. At a very low volume.

Again, I have to say, I really like your individuality. All kindness and light and loyalty. Or, so I imagine. *(Moves toward her, perhaps at some point stepping off-stage and out of the light. He is, at times, aware of the audience, and is at times self-conscious about having this conversation.)* Maybe you could meet me, later on? After? I don't know where I'll be, so maybe don't bother. Unless you'd like to. We'll get a drink. Who knows. Depending on how terrible your life is, I could be a good move for you. Maybe I didn't have to say all that. *(He returns to the stage.)* And I may have plans anyway. So forget I said anything. Or imagined you at all. Forget I thought or felt anything.

(Returning to general audience.) So, the woman. Of our story. No, let's forget the woman for a little while, if we could. Let me jump around here. Thanks. Let's get back to the inner child. The crippled kid with the electrocuted dog. Did I say his face was disfigured? Even if I hadn't, can you picture the face of a little boy in your mind, without disfiguring it anyway? Can you picture anything without it falling apart? Can you picture even a simple square without it going sideways and wrong and triangular? *(Very brief pause. "Noticing" that an audience member is experiencing the mental image*

of a square going sideways in his or her mind.) Like that. I'm not
sure you can. Anyway, let's forge ahead, despite our obvious
flaws. I'm speaking to the obviously flawed among us. And, as
well, to those of us whose deformations are more private. *(To
a person in third or fourth row, to whom THOM has not yet spoken.)*
Hello, sir.

So, the boy. Becoming a man, in the puddle. Or, no, we're
farther along than that.

It's late. He comes home, a dark house. Walks up the stairs,
supperless. Something is amiss. Some real thing is amiss.
Though who could put a finger on it, in it, who could see it
and state it plainly, the trouble in the bone-quiet nights in the
tidy house on Garden Street? Having seen the boy, the only-
child, make his way from room to room, in search of anything
to mother or sister him? I dare say no one. The personality
forms in the dark. This is possibly a very good point. The
worldview arises at night, without witness. The boy's did,
as he grew, changed, away from people, in the bathroom,
in the rain, down halls in everyday familial places. I dare
say…no I don't. I do know they didn't pat his head. They
didn't muss up his hair and say, Good Boy. He comes and
goes, untouched, his childhood running out, as he becomes a
foreigner, an immigrant to the place where he was born.

To a man wearing a regular and common shirt in the audience.

I have that same shirt.

Anyway. That night, the night of the stormy day that was
his dead dog's last, that night he had, with his brutal new
haircut, a wet dream, or, nocturnal emission, if you like. Who
knows what he dreamt of. Some inscrutably human thing,
no doubt. Something out of the vocabulary and wilderness
of a little boy at night. Maybe of a woman bending over,
knees-deep in muddy water, a scribbled picture of a scribbled
feeling. Or maybe of some fuzzy uneducated image of a girl,

saying a word he liked. "Voucher." Or, "Ankles." Whispering one of those funny little words that only refer to words, like "Such." Maybe he just felt some felicific little twinge, a nice little physical feeling in the night, and came, without language. His little bed and the little sheets with airplanes on them are covered in semen and freshly badly-cut hair. What a mysterious scene. And somewhere in the same night another youth bleeds between her legs, staring out a window, wondering whom to tell, wondering what to tell them. What a mystery. The onset of the breeding years. Growth. The cancers are almost all in place. Nature laughs last, ladies and gentlemen, laughs hardest and best and last, deep into the night, at you. *(Gently, softly, solemnly.)* But, think of it all. What a paradise, as I have said. What a surprise to have a body.

Meaning, across the world, hardly anyone sleeps. How could they? Every night spent in the body is a fitful night. Fighting gravity, and losing. Night after fitful night spent fighting everything.

But so that morning, the messy morning of the messy night, that morning on a walk through a meadow, the boy was attacked by bees. A nest had fallen onto the ground and he had kicked it by accident, his eyes shut because of the sun and maybe some other reason he had. *(A momentary departure from the story:)* Is it clear I love my little subject, and therefore don't pry too hard into his reasons, his empty head, his stupid little agenda on earth? Anyway, the bees. They swarmed into his eyes and mouth, stung him on every skinny surface. The boy did not, at first, make any sound. The poor thing did not understand. He thought, out in the meadow, that he had done something wrong. He thought that the pain was already in his body and was only coming out then to punish him, that the bees had only happened along later and were trying to help. His body was exploding in painful sores, which the bees were trying to salve, to soothe. This, according to him. He really didn't understand things. Kind of beautiful, if you like that sort of thing. If you like the idea of a little boy desperately spreading stinging bees over his bleeding body. Desperately yelling "Help me, Bees, Help," and putting his little swollen hand into the hive for more.

Pause.

We've all made similar mistakes. Mistaking the bee for the flower, giving our heart away to the first prick or bitch to come down the trickling river. Anyway, the boy crawled enough away, almost died, lay there until evening, neither crying nor laughing, a thing of nature, in pain among the crickets and frogs.

Pause.

So that's the bee incident.

Pause.

I have an incredibly rich interior life.

A long pause. Thirty seconds, a minute. THOM PAIN regards the audience. Perhaps he stares for a moment at the woman in the audience to whom he has been speaking. He does almost nothing, just stands there, living his rich interior life.

Yeah.

Brief pause.

You really are very forgiving. To let me get lost like this. No one else lets me do anything. Everyone else always has these little tips, different ideas about ways I could be. "Hey, what about a haircut? Must you be exactly that tall? Maybe you could talk different. Why are you looking east? Brush your teeth. Change. I hate how you breathe." *(Brief pause.)*

On the last couple lines above, THOM PAIN has perhaps inadvertently shown how others have treated him, how the world has felt to him. He tries to move into a gentle and more forgiving mode.

So, comparatively, you really are a nice group. So easygoing, watching so gently. Looking out at you all, I am struck by the sort of –

He fixes on a woman in the audience.

Is that – Sarah? Is it you? I can't believe it.

Almost immediately.

Mary?

He moves a few steps.

Next, I'm going to do this:

He pulls out a handkerchief and blows his nose. As he's putting it away, he sees something in its folds that gives him an idea.

Behold. Consider. Use your head and imagine this is a brain. Or, the mind. There it is, in the skull of a boy still in the womb, battleship gray and growing, folding over on itself, turning, as he kicks his way into the world. Amazing. A little boy learns to crawl, the nerves firing, his mind relying on his hands and knees. A less-little boy is introduced to a stranger, is embarrassed, his brain sending blood to his face, his mind telling him, "Look down, little boy. Hurt inside. Be shy." And so on and on. Until an old man sits in a chair, the hearing gone, the eyes gone, the body almost gone – but the brain still going, or the mind, insisting on itself, making itself heard, causing trouble. There, the brain, the mind, in a chair, in a field, or under stars, in the bright sun of Egypt, Beantown, Whoville, all the while all the while fighting, revising, planning its next defeat. Or a man stands before you, age unimportant, the mouth moving, big things going badly, but a million little things going right – the brain is doing its job. But, the mind, another story. It's a monster. They don't know, the doctors, the distinguished authors. But, oh, the memories up there. Her fine hand on your shoulder, on the steps of a museum. The dog at play, with a caterpillar. Insomnia, nausea, ocean waves. The taste of mascara, the feeling of night, how the world can sound. Such a feeling life, such sensation, yes? Then pile the words on top. And watch them seep down. Think of it. The brain and the mind. All that up there. Married, happily or not. Imagine.

Pause.

Or just think about snot. Mucus. Imagine that this is a handkerchief. And that I just blew my nose into it.

He balls up the handkerchief and, with a magician's flourish, puts it back in his pocket.

To backtrack: you worry, you have anxiety, the blood vessels constrict, the handkerchief crumples, it's a headache, a migraine, a blow to the head, and now you try to live. It all seems so useless, so unusable. The house that you live in, the oceans, the mountains, the peace-keeping forces. The restaurants and anniversaries, the factories and gardens, useless. Fuck it all, kill it and burn it all down, you say, if you have a little headache.

So maybe I have a little headache. Maybe I was born with a little headache. Maybe this is all. Just some wrong pressure somewhere. I'm speaking softly for a reason. I guess because I hope that you... I don't know.

Pause.

Let's go over the enormous and informative ground we've covered so far. We were talking – or, I guess I was talking – about a little girl – a little boy I guess it was – who got stung by a bee and used to have a dog. Then, about falling in love – remember? We all went back in time. Or, I did. Then I took out a handkerchief, tried to use my imagination on you. I think that brings us up to now.

Pause.

Okay. Did the raffle, did the joke about the horse. Oh, I know. Another joke. Why is an old lady like a tiny motorcycle? *(He waits for a moment, to see if anyone has an answer.)* Well, of course, she isn't, she isn't at all. You should be disgusted with yourself for even for a second trying to think of how she might be. I'm disgusted with myself. And this makes me, you know, act out. Lash out. *(Quietly.)* Or lash in.

But, to continue. The woman, my darling, from earlier. One fine week, we woke to cold sores tearing through our lips. Picture that we lay in bed: me, confused and not unhappy; her, thinking thoughts I never knew, never will. We were so full of life, each other. "Love cankers all." A pun – Thank you. She had beautiful eyes – I must have looked. And I bet she smiled, or tried to, through the cracking pain, the dryness I caused in her.

It was more complicated than this, our love. Plus, I lied about all of it. But it was a while back, all some time ago – maybe this morning. Or even longer back, early this morning. The poem of the wee-most hours. The old stars twinkle over the scene. No one else in sight. Bony stray dogs roam the street. Stars and dogs circle our house, us asleep in love, or wide awake. One or the other.

It makes you stop and think. These timeless times. How long does everything take? How long did I kiss her, the time I lost track of time, my lips red with life, saying nothing, covering her in me, in my saliva? And how long did our little hero, who I'm getting sick of, lay there in the meadow drooling, in bed, or, in the park, which we'll get to? Long enough, I should think. Long enough to learn something.

But back to the cold sores. After all my efforts at communication, something had passed between us. Would that I might provoke in you a similar mark, a little growth, a blemish of real life. Don't think that I think I will. *(To a particular man or woman in the audience.)* Any thoughts? Feelings? *(Immediately, but somehow gently.)* I'm sure. *(To audience.)* Anyway. The woman and the man, myself. Good good times. Except for all of our unfixable problems, everything was perfect. Epic romance in the aisles of all-night stores. Unaloneness, at last, the stupid clouds lift. Kissing in the morning, pissing together in the roomy handicapped bathrooms of the emptier museums. A million little weddings. My life to this point was mishaps. I was just accidents and wrong roads before her. But, then, the lost was found. Happiness. Perfection, with an asterisk. Yes, she found my desire a little unruly, a little dire, too much of an emergency. And I don't know how well the family ghosts got along. But in the intermingling of our – well, not intermingling, exactly. I don't know. *(Brief pause. Sadly, solemnly.)* We've all probably had the roughly same experience. Yes?

Maybe a little frustrated with the audience's response, or lack of response.

You're looking at me like you've, like you've never even...

He sticks his tongue out a bit, and grabs it a couple times with his thumb and finger. He looks at his hand and then grabs his tongue a couple more times. He removes whatever was bothering him. Quietly, almost to himself:

Hair. Human.

Brief pause. He looks at us.

Back to the boy, then, the little mistake. He's grown into a bigger mistake. Aching bones from the growth spurts, furious oily skin, shy to the point of not even really being there. He watched the parade of life go by. Drew some faulty conclusions. He said almost nothing. No one ever asked him what he was thinking, so he never really got into the habit.

Though it came later, anyway.

I sometimes like to think.

Though this wasn't always the case.

(He stares, and mainly remains staring, lost in the feelings and images.) I'm thinking right now. Yeah. I am. We were the perfect height. Look at me think. We must have been so stunning. Will I be awake when I die? What luck, to be me, then, with her. The dirty nights, the magic days at the Laundromat. Sharing forks, taking our clothes off, afraid of nothing, we felt. *(Returning his attention to the audience.)* I disappeared in her and she, wondering where I went, left. It's not clear what happened, exactly.
So you just try to…

Do you like magic? I do. I think. It's fairly ambivalent, this love of mine.

Pause.

Once a moth was flying around my room. I was afraid. A yucky flapping moth. And me. It all had some effect, I'm sure. End of rumination. Thank you very much.

Now, I'm going to need, not a volunteer, but, a subject, from the audience. Don't raise your hands shouting "Me, Me." Though, certainly, I see your point. I'll choose someone. We know who you are. It'd be good if the person were wearing light clothing. If he or she spoke a second language and liked a little violence, that'd be great. So, let's see.

He is looking through the audience. The house lights come up (somewhat jerkily, as if the stage manager was not aware that any of this was going to happen), as he moves into the aisle, surveying the faces. He may move deep into the house. On some lines, he speaks directly to a particular person. He is relaxed and conversational, which, given the context, should heighten the sense of threat and menace.

I apologize for this, we all hate things like this. But in order
for me to fully prove my point, to really ram the thing home,
I need a subject. A volunteer, really. One of you watchers.
One of you lovely pounding hearts. Now. Who, who, who.

Or, whom.

I sounded like an owl just then. Anyway. How about this
recent weather. You know? What a day to be outside. Hi.
I saw someone walking eight dogs today. All so pretty,
so pedigreed, except for one ugly mutt, a runt, angry and
diseased, less loved ergo less loveable. *(He crouches a little,
or kneels, to get a particular view of the stage.)* This is good
seat. I hope you're paying attention. I am – because of my
own pains – going to make someone else suffer, without
proportion. Because this is your reality and not my dream,
because I miss her leg around my neck, someone is going to
pay. Nice. The leashes were all tangled.
I really apologize. But. So. Now. Our volunteer, our conscript.
Anyone will do, but it has to be someone. *(He moves down to
stand in front of the audience.)* Who of you deserves it most?
I see you. Who shall join me? I see a couple people are game.

*Long pause. He looks around at the faces one more time. Perhaps
he is too afraid to go through with it, or, perhaps he has not found
anyone worthy, and feels that he – no matter how seriously he's being
taken – is not being taken seriously enough.*

You know what – skip it. *(Earnestly.)* Thank you, though.

*Pause. He glances at his watch, thinks a bit. Begins to move back
onto the stage. House lights down.*

So…

Pause. A quiet but fraught moment. He commits to continuing.

So life for the little boy, now a little man, sped up and sped
up. He was schooled, to no effect, and left home, saying only,

"I'm going somewhere else now." His mother wept, due to an unrelated malady. His father, who is still alive, God rest his soul, waved goodbye. And so, our young man, to a city. He got jobs. You may have seen him, something close enough. He's the man waving the flag that says PARKING, next to a sign that says PARKING. He's dressed as a telephone, handing out flyers concerning telephones. He's picking up trash, eating in doorways, eyes down, an expressionless expression. He's just like you, or, is you, or he isn't and doesn't like you. See the former child, hated by life, about my size, losing weight, working for shit pay, no real belongings other than a dictionary.

One night, picture it a winter night, one night in a park, walking off the day's food poisoning, he came upon some vomit, vomited, and then collapsed. He wondered, as he shivered on the freezing ground, covered in stomach fluid, saliva, and bile, if there might be, you know, more to life than this. Nearby, a brightly-lit skating rink. He lay there, in the slush, listening to Christmas music and chirping elegies to reindeer and snow. The shivers of his childhood came, and then stopped. He got up and went over to the rink, leaned on the side. Families glided by. Couples. Call it the Christmas spirit, call it a coincidence, call it whatever you like, but, suddenly, in the bright light and beautiful music, he got sick and collapsed again.

That next day, at the city morgue, where he was painting the bathrooms, he saw a woman in a dark dress and black hat. He felt alive and high on the fumes. He watched her cry. She was perfect in her grief. A born widow, or orphan, a person of serious and recent loss. You can guess the rest, so I could leave it at that, but I'll tell you. She didn't see him, never would, and that was the end of that. I probably shouldn't have even mentioned it. But it was a start.

Pause. He looks into the audience. Quietly:

You're a nice-looking crowd. I see we have some couples here tonight. And on came the animals, two by two. Good for you. *(Very brief pause.)* Really, good for you.

Brief pause.

Anyway, a few seasons later, picture him sitting nowhere really, a nice day in terms of weather, reading his dictionary like a novel, scanning ahead to see if the story picks up. Remember, the man is the boy, from earlier. He is not really outfitted for this life, not properly clothed, not enough skin. He reads on, absently picking a scab on the side of his head, staring at the word "veneer." Suddenly, like a beautiful dog at the wrong door, or, a gentle snow in the morning, or, no, just an unexpected natural thing, she appeared. She appears.

THOM looks off, toward a door, as if She has just walked in. He pauses. Looks elsewhere, then looks down and pauses, again, before continuing quietly with the following realization.

Sometimes you look off somewhere. There's something you want to see. You expect this almost operatic moment to happen in your life, you expect something to appear. And all that's there is what was there before. And you, looking. And what do you do? Maybe there *was* a raffle. Maybe we all won. Or, all lost, together. I'm speaking softly again. Because I want to be heard. Because I want to be gentle. To be, to my own self, untrue.

In a very small gesture, he shakes his head slowly; perhaps he can't believe what his life has come to, how impossible his simple wants and needs seem.

Here she comes. The one everyone would agree was the one. Not the widow, not a widow, but close. A modesty, an understanding, a pain, a complication. A human being. Imagine a gazelle, a zebra, a giraffe. Now don't imagine any more animals, and picture a woman. Another person.

God, if you could see her. Imagine he is not afraid. Imagine he has feelings. Imagine he reaches in his pocket. "Pick a card," he says. "There's only one," she says, demurely, womanlyly. "Yeah," he says, in customary brevity, but surprising coherence. Anyone could see. Off they went. To Laundromats, chapels, and bathrooms, places you've heard of, been to yourself. The steps of museums. Hand in hand in hand in hand. She would write him letters, one of which he would save. Love, period, full stop, probably. Unless you're very happy or have a good imagination, you can't imagine how happy they were. They were very close. Not fully there, but close. We hear the word love a lot, throw it around. Less and less maybe but still a lot. The word love. We mean all sorts of things. *(Very brief pause. He is perhaps distracted by the revelation of his immense failure in life, in love, in his ability to understand.)* I don't know. It's really…on this freezing…how anybody…or we were probably…damn it. *(Brief pause.)* He couldn't see the story through. He did not love too much, nor too well, but with too much sweat, shit, and fear, with too many long words, too many commas. It seems. *(Brief pause.)* May every animal find its animal. Find some food, its fellow animal, a warm rock and somewhere dark to sleep.

Though still restrained, THOM is more vulnerable and open than we have previously seen.

Where are we supposed to learn about things? What happens in the little spurt? In the little time we are, I guess, given?

Brief pause. From his breast pocket, he removes an old envelope, from which he removes an old letter.

Maybe this'll explain.

He prepares to read the letter aloud. He looks at it for a few moments.

Nope.

Pause. He turns his back to the audience for a moment, as he figures

*out what to do next, and, if he has the courage to do it. THOM goes
upstage to the folding chair. He brings it downstage and opens it up.*

I just got this. From back there.

I don't like magic, I'm no good at it, and I don't like it, but I
do do a little Disappearing Act. I'll need another volunteer.
Seriously, no kidding around, this time. *(Steps into the audience.
To a man in the front row.)* Thank you. May I? You'll do fine.
Thank you.

*THOM brings a man onstage from the audience. He leads him to
the folding chair he has set up and has him stand next to it. THOM
might also ask him to sit down in the chair, to make the person more
comfortable so he doesn't return to the audience.*

The Disappearing Act. Here we go. *(To man onstage.)* Maybe
you could just – no, this is fine. Now, close your eyes. You
have to completely trust that I'm not going to – *(He takes a few
steps downstage, speaking as he moves, leaving the person behind him,
upstage.)* Do you know, she came back to me, sort of. I had the
worst dream, the other night. I'll spare you the details. And the
main parts. But when I woke up, I went out for a walk.

I liked the weather. It was nice out, sort of raining. I could see
myself in people's dark windows. I stopped thinking and just
let everything come. Let the words run. They came and went,
disappeared. Like the things they stood for. Like they're doing now.

My face was so swollen. I saw white clouds in the still
puddles. Her pretty ankles, dresses she wore. I lay there. I lay
everywhere, always looking up. I miss her so much. I miss my
mom and dad. I miss how the dog's fur felt in the winter on a
school night. *I do, I do. Help me, bees, help. I'm going somewhere
else now.* I was born in a brick building on a Wednesday
afternoon. Was that really me, before, in the dark, trying to
make the matches work, trying to get to sleep, holding on to
an oven mitt? She said I love you. My eyes were closed, the

sun being bright. I heard buzzing and said I love you. Creak, creak. He said to me, Sarah? Mary? Who did he think I was? Is anyone up here? Weeping mother, waving father, shivering dog, paper cut-out doll. I sniffed butterflies. I pissed on things. Oh, you. My poor face. We tried with him, we really did. This is my best friend. Who am I, now, and what difference does it make? Who was I then? I cut my hair half off. I bled in the night. I left home but I never did, but I didn't stay. I wasn't anywhere. Then I was in love. *(Brief pause.)* Now I'm here.

Pause.

You're being very patient.

Wherever THOM has gone, it has taken something out of him. He makes some small efforts at getting himself back together: wipes his nose, rubs his eyes. Then speaks to the woman in the audience to whom he has earlier spoken.

We might have had something together. Wouldn't that have been nice. Off go the animals, two by two. Love.

To the audience, simply, quietly.

I was lucky in it, once. I wanted to leave before I was left. She wanted it that way, or would, soon enough. Maybe. I never understood things. I was too confusing. I did everything in fear. In fear of fear. What was I so afraid of? I had promise. I don't have anything anymore.

He moves upstage, gets a drink of water, and returns. A quick glance out to the audience without looking toward the man on stage.

(To man onstage.) I thought you would have left by now. What do you want? Not to disappear, I'm sure. Then, what? *(He moves toward him, with the glass of water.)* Shall I love you slowly and be true? Shall I stroke your cheek, gently, almost not at all, and bring you – *(Very loudly, to scare him.)* Boo! *(THOM is somewhat surprised and frightened too.)* Sorry. Have my

glass of water. Your throat must be getting dry, from all the things you'll never say.

THOM hands him the glass of water. To audience, again, humbly, gently.

Then there's you. Don't say anything. Don't think anything. Just be yourself. Keep in mind how little time there is, how little time there always was. Then try to be brave. Try to be someone else. Someone better.

Ffff. Ffff. Eeearr. A word without definition. "Fear." Nothing to be afraid of. Beautiful. Right? So the little boy, somewhat hilariously, was never able – *(Very loudly, a final howl, not very clearly enunciated:)* Boo! *(Again, THOM is surprised, even scared by this "Boo." Maybe it's the death throe of his former cruel self?)* Sorry again. Why do I do that? Enough. I have to go. You have to go. Maybe someone is waiting. Please be someone waiting. I'm done with this. Important things will happen, now. I promise. Be stable, be stable, be stable, be stable.

Brief pause. THOM moves toward the man onstage, stands and stares at him, as if challenging him to act, to respond. THOM softens in his stance, and, pats the man tenderly but awkwardly on the elbow. THOM moves a few steps downstage to speak to the audience.

I know this wasn't much, but, let it be enough. Do. *(Spoken normally and quietly.)* Boo. *(Brief pause.)* Isn't it great to be alive?

Lights down, with perhaps the last fading light on the volunteer before all go to black.

End.

Stage Properties

A match, a piece of paper, a watch, an unlightable cigarette, a chair, a handkerchief, a wrinkled envelope containing a wrinkled letter, a pitcher of water, a water glass, perhaps a small table. Maybe Thom has stashed a can of soda with a straw in it, somewhere on the stage, in order to have a quick drink while he's making a point or staring at the audience.

General production notes

Everything about the production should be as simple as possible, with all of the work and attention being concentrated on the actor and his performance. There is a humility about theatre and life, in the script; it should be there in the production, too. Gratuitous light or sound effects, or scenery, would disable this humility and confuse the play, making the overall experience less forceful. Though subtle lighting effects, it should be said, can be used to great effect. Though these lighting effects should be, as with most other production choices, almost unnoticeable, felt more than seen.

General performance notes

The actor should, of course, be so comfortable and familiar with the script that the words come out of him as if they are his own, as if he is making them up as he goes along. It is mainly feeling, rather than thought, that is behind the words: fear, anxiety, heartache, desire, love, hate. There are a lot of "switch-backs" and changes-of-direction in the script. He thinks and feels quickly and changes his mind often; we all do. All directions that Thom might go in are true, each direction comes out of a real feeling and a real need to move in that particular direction at that particular time. Thom feels and believes almost everything he says, at the moment that he says it. Sometimes, the feeling changes-- simple as that. Though there are many parts of play that are meant to be humorous, for the most part, Thom is unaware or unconcerned that what he is saying might be found funny. He is serious, he is trying. He is, to use a dangerous word, sincere-- sincere in his disgust, sincere in his sympathy;

sincere in his desire to make a connection with the audience, and, sincere in his frustration when he cannot. People feel a lot of things, a lot of things at the same time, sometimes opposing things at the same time. The actor should honor this, honor the largeness, the complicatedness, of human beings, and find a way to play it all as simply and truly as possible. Thom has suffered all of the pains and hurt that he describes the boy in the story suffering, and so he is wounded, and so he will tell the boy's story with real authority. This authority should give the performance, along with naturalness and ease, a somewhat heightened and somewhat cold and formal style of delivery. This, Thom's repression of his feelings, his refusal to show everything that is inside of him, will create a tension. Thom is hardened, angry, and perhaps he is going to inflict some of the pain he knows onto the audience. But not just for the sake of being cruel. All that he has suffered has made him sensitive, in some secret part of himself, to others' suffering, to the suffering in the Universe. He wants to make his life mean something, to turn the ruination of his life into a salvation, into something noble, for himself and for the audience. It is recommended that at some point, later in rehearsals, the actor begins to work with an audience. Thom needs something from them, as they do from him, and, he has something he wants to give them, and these things will become clearer when Thom is confronted with an audience, and an audience is confronted with Thom.

There should be a manic energy to the performance, so that we are never really sure which way Thom is going to go. Though this manic energy should be covered by a layer of intense and severe (often cold) formality.

Finally, it is very important that Thom Pain is never pissy, bored, or overly cerebral. He is not even ever mean. Cruel, perhaps, but not mean. He is solemn and grave, often, and can be this way almost effortlessly. He feels large and powerful feelings, which he is usually able to convert into language, or, cover or deny with language. Or a change of topic. We should feel and see Thom's feelings much more in their suppression than in their expression. We should feel the almost relentless pressure of them, as with the soda can that has been violently shaken. There it sits. Will it explode? Did we just see it trembling?

LADY GREY
(in ever-lower light)

DRAMATIS PERSONAE

LADY GREY, possibly British

Setting: A theatre
Stage Properties: A chair
Wardrobe: A simple dress

LADY GREY

Lights up on LADY GREY. She regards audience, very still, as if watching a play or, say, in a difficult conversation with a friend, waiting for him to speak. Pause.

You seem nervous, so, why don't I start.

How many are we? *(She quickly counts audience, reckons with figure briefly.)* You looked like fewer people.

Pause.

But, thank you for coming. It doesn't work, my life, without people sitting there, staring, undressing me with their eyes, then undressing themselves, brushing their teeth in their minds and falling asleep, wishing they were dead. So, honestly, thank you.

I'll begin.

'Show-and-tell?' Do we have any familiarity with the term? If not, allow me. Here we go, and I'll go slow– not wanting to leave any of you behind, until such time as I– you know– do. So, Show-and-tell: Tradition of the latter days of the waning years of the North American school system. Child brings object into school, a rock he likes or a photo of herself, is called on by the teacher, moves to the front of the room, stands there shaking and childlike, shows object, discourses on same for a few mumbly minutes, closes disappointingly, having forgotten the important parts, managing not to cry, or to only cry a little, and sits back down. And so forward throughout the North American day, rocks and photos, nothing much, keepsakes and little animals, teeth that fell out, an interesting scar. Occasionally, some overachiever with a bodily organ, his tonsils or appendix, floating in a jar of formaldehyde, proudly held aloft, nothing much to add. 'Thank you very much, please sit back down.' Show-and-tell

helps the child apply language to an object, to see if it sticks.
Helps the child grow in his ability to convey an inner reality,
assuming any of those words applies. Also, gives the tired
teacher a day off, nothing to prepare, he or she can sit back
like you and watch the stream of little crap, hear the stream
of little sentences, the human human *ums* and *ohs* and *I-don't-
knows*. All meant to express the dearness of the shown object,
a dearness that remains, in most cases, unexpressed. There's
something impossible about it. Something soft and accidental.
Real. In this simple little structure. That's all.

Brief pause. Regards audience.

Bravo. Let me guess— an 'audience,' right? Or, wait, no—
'friends of the deceased?' 'Family of the victim?' White
people in chairs. Cheer up. You're all very beautiful, in a very
general way. Smile.

Brief pause.

'Um. Oh. I don't know.'

You do all look so nice. In this very low light.

Now.

Pause.

My childhood was, what should we say, humanistic. Not that
anyone asked. But, yes, it gave the impression of a childhood,
while it was going by. Like anyone's, I don't doubt. All
the bells and whistles, a generally screaming age, skinned
knees and girlish pain. I look back on my childhood, in the
evenings. I think of things I could have said. I try to picture
old things, people's faces, feelings, get drunk on nostalgia,
alcohol. Which leaves me my mornings free, to do with
as I despise or like. To recover from the wasted night, do
dishes, lacerate the woman back into the girl. I try to read
or do watercolors, sinking sidewise and deeper into the life

we all agree we thought we would avoid. Do I gather from your polite lack of response that we have some kind of understanding? A little sympathy, do I sense in the silence? Or just a polite lack of response. I could never differentiate.

Brief pause.

A girl needs a name, doesn't she. Jennifer should do, Jen. So. Jennifer has brown hair, completely arresting and sparkling dark– you know what, you've seen a girl before. Jennifer is the girl you see when someone says 'girl.' She is walking home from school, as she suddenly appears in our story, thinking about her assignment, show-and-tell tomorrow. She is walking past houses, through wheatfields, men watching her pass, then a wide empty road, a pretty dress, she is girly, the days getting shorter. I see this in a rural sort of setting, autumnal. It could happen anywhere, anytime. But I give you waving wheatfields, blue skies, a girl walking through them, under them. I give you horseflies and falling leaves. *(Very brief pause.)* You're welcome. We see her blink slowly, push her hair behind her ears. I don't know why.

Brief pause.

She is thinking about her life, possibly.

Brief pause.

I like drama.

Longer pause.

You too, I can tell.

Jennifer. A girl, a body, alive in the night and morning. See the girl. You understand what it means to be human. Jen is keeping busy around the house, being human.

There is nothing we need to pretend.

Brief pause.

I caught the acting bug when I was very young. Maybe it was just a rash. The doctors said it was all in my head. Then they said it had spread to my spine. Me and my acting bug, my metal back brace, dreams of treading the boards, eight years old, unable to walk. It turned out to be something viral, something you just get. People came by, stared, told me what I was missing, gave me the homework, filled me in. It hurt all the time but it hurt differently. A little variety, in the laming. I couldn't do this. *(She takes two steps.)* I couldn't even do this. *(She takes one step.)* I could barely do this. *(She does nothing. Pause. Slight bow.)* Thank you. Needless to say, as I say it anyway, if someone came by to quote visit, I couldn't move, I couldn't run away. And so I bore the attentions of your fellow human beings, on my back in the afternoons in a dark house.

Brief pause.

Oh, the miracle of walking, of flight, the beauty of running screaming. And, ah, the miracle of standing still. Be grateful, movers. Shakers. This too, this mobility, shall pass.

Brief pause.

So there I was, in bed, and younger. I began to see myself as watchable. It was here, these months, semi-paralyzed and abed, that I was able, in my pain, to hone a skill for something or other. It was from in this position that I learned that the world was something I might lie down for, holding my nose while it enacted its worldliness on me. Similar revelations, anyone? Like hardships? Trouble in the bedroom— shooting pain, shame, paralysis? I'm sure. But you take the bad with the good, ride out the difference. You'll have some failures, sure, but then you get sick and die. It evens out, yes? I continue, ladylike, but unconcerned with your reply. Which is not to say I don't need you. Just not really right now.

You could compare me to a summer's day, though this really

wouldn't be necessary. I could be compared to a winter's night, too, though by whom, and why? I'm like last Saturday. Cold, cloudy, over. I can't be bothered.

I can be bothered, I lied.

Life is shocking.

Unreadiness is all.

Pause.

Does anyone know what I need someone to do, right now, quickly? No? It's not your fault. That you do not hear what I will not say. But, isn't it? Yes, this is small of me. But so is this: Die, every single one of you, twice. A cancer on all your houses.

I'm sorry.

Anyway, I wouldn't worry. I've cursed people before. It never seems to stick.

Pause.

Jennifer, we hardly know you.

Pause.

Do I seem familiar? I'm looking at you, with something in mind. Can you stand it? Some people can't. Some people run for the hills. When I say hills, I don't think of whatever hills you think of. We can try to overcome that. The fact that we use the same words for things but don't have the same things for the words. We all think our mothers are named Mother. We may try to specify: Mom, Momma, Mommy, Mummy, Maman, Mum, Ma. To make her feel special, less anonymous. She is merely the thing that gets the name. The body that drifted through the word. Like the woman before you. Who is not familiar.

I have nice eyes. Dark and sparkling. It is said. Compelling,
up to a point. I think these were the words. What do you
think? What can you tell me about you? I ask the question—
what's the word— rhetorically.

Pause.

I'm with you in your anger, your disappointment, or, quote,
whatever. Are you with me, in mine? Where does it come
from, think you? This overriding feeling, this smoldering
something. Have you your hunches? As have others before
you, who had theirs? Who would, after dismounting, smoke,
have their hunches, give their notes on my performance as a
woman lying down, put on their shoes and then leave. Others
might not have been so— what's the word— as I was. Others
might have been even more whatever-the-word-is than I was.
I was desperate and confused. I will be again. I don't know.
Who knows. You don't.

You're not the first. Or the last.

I've been looked at, sized up, pored over, before.

There was an American— or Canadian, I don't know, one of
those grain-producing countries. American, I'm starting to
have the feeling. Decent-enough, polite to a fault, also brown
hair, seething with rage, hate, average height, promising at
tennis. I felt everything with him, for a while. On a scale of
1 to 3— with 3 being only slightly different from 1— he was,
I don't know. In the end? Honestly? Just a blue shirt. Some
dark sunglasses.

Brief pause.

I loved that shirt. The grown man hiding in it, hunkering
down, making his life in it? Never was I to really know. 'Fine,'
he'd say, if asked how he was. 'I'm fine,' his mouth would
say, him shaking with some untold pain, some resolvable
problem, me staring at myself in his sunglasses. Understater.

Leaver. Mouse. 'Fine.' He was a clumsy man. My tireless efforts in pointing this out did nothing to make him more graceful. He cried constantly, or said nothing. If he talked he talked about the weather, but he never seemed willing to do anything about it. He would stare at me, blankly, waiting, and I would tell him to stop. He would. Fine. The way I go on, you'd think that I was born with minty fresh breath, that I grew money under my arms. No, I had my imperfections. Sometimes, pouring myself into bed, I missed. Sometimes, I woke up shouting, enraged at him for some deficiency in my dreams, or a creak he made the stairs make. Some nights, while he was clumsily trying to express himself, I had trouble pretending I was asleep. I stormed out of places, left-in-the-night sort of thing. Sometimes, I waited all day to leave in the night. I made the most of the silence he provided, and filled it with gory fantasies of betrayal and hate, scenes in which we punished each other, in which I came out, bloodily, on top. I was pretty ugly, sometimes. Still, I have my charms, my qualities.

Pause. She assumes 'ballet, fourth position.'

I studied dance. *(Brief pause. She returns to a normal stance.)* Then I quit.

I can sing, if you made me. If you– you know– if you put a gun to my head.

Brief pause.

No guns here, tonight, I guess? How very English. Not even some lone drunk with a rusted box-cutter or razor blade in his pocket, to encourage me in my singing career. Well, it's the thought that counts.

Pause. Sings.

'In the jungle, the mighty jungle…'

'Do, a deer, a female deer; re, a drop of golden sun; mi, a name I call myself; fa, a long long way to run.'

Speaks.

Why don't we forget the singing.

Long pause.

I was thinking about something else.

Brief pause.

Does this ever happen to you? *(Brief pause.)* You're looking for something, a word or some old toy. Something by which you will be revealed, expressed. Wondering what the story of yourself is, and, how to tell it. And why. It did, to her. Jen. Rejected items would include: a dead aunt's radio, a dead dog's dog tag, two pieces of glass, and a toy watch. Also, a candle from her baptism, something papery from Japan, an old photo of a man on a horse. All seeming to Joanne– or, Jen, whoever– not-enough-her for her. Her not knowing this is an art of diction and feeling, not objects and props, her not knowing any old thing, a paper clip, a dirty bed sheet, a dog collar, would do just as well as anything else, provided her heart was in it.

There she is, rummaging through her life. A girl versus the world, coming to terms with what is not in it for her. She is all alone. Look close. See another person clearly. It's just me, here. Armed with what? Reassured by what? A chair? Take a moment out of your busy life to admire my simple dress.

Pause.

There are different kinds of silence. You know the distinction. The silence before someone is going to say something. The silence before someone isn't.

She opens her mouth almost imperceptibly, about to speak, stops. Pause.

Which one was that, I wonder. As we continue in this tale. Of life. The sum of forces that resist death. Life: about which we have all heard and read a great deal, I'm sure.

Pause.

Do you want me to take my clothes off?

Immediately.

I thought so.

Pause.

Jennifer is walking to school, through the Americas, the Western Hemisphere, wherever– empty-handed. Long years of family life, time on earth, experience, and, nothing to show. Are birds singing, on a telephone wire? Is there an airplane in the overly blue sky? Is something moving in the bushes? Does she shiver, wishing she were gone? *(Brief pause.)* I don't know, you tell me.

One day, he told me he was leaving forever, and came back with cigarettes. When he said he was going out for cigarettes, I thought I understood, but he came back with flowers and milk. We did laugh, sometimes. I opened up to him somewhat. We tried to tell each other about ourselves. He liked to look at my face. In a crowded park on a sunny day, he said, 'I love you. Watch this,' and turned and walked away. I followed, out of curiosity, hurt, watched him turn corners, double back, saw the second-thoughts, the third-thoughts in his walk, tried keeping up until I lost him or interest and sat down near a fountain.

And so was that, ladies and gentlemen, that?

A minor loss, comparatively. A pretty shirt. People come and go. Mothers die. Hard lessons, in which nothing is learned. Fill in your own blanks.

I'd like to talk about suicide, but, am afraid one or more of
you would laugh, yell something mean, try to discourage
me from the idea. Of raising such a serious topic, on such
a laughable evening. Don't lose hope, maybe later. But, if
someone were to yell something hurtful, that would help me
really feel it, really help me be 'in the moment,' and that's
surely what we all want. A moment, and somebody in it. I
don't know. Here I am.

I should stop here.

Brief pause.

And start here.

A girl. Born, of a winter, a mother, crying, and why not?
Was scared. Overcame. Was overcome, and, scared again;
ruined, effectively. Any worse than anyone else? Who knows.
But certainly differently, individually. The things people do
to people. The little years better-never-mentioned. Or, just,
never mentioned. Or hardly. But to continue, rose again.
Tried to stand before her fellow man. Tried and tried. To find
love, in any of its forms, even if only fleeting, even if not
even love. She sang, danced, spoke, stopped. Ailed. Prayed,
for the hell of it. Flailed against her fellow men. Dabbled in
thoughts of the above, grew in her inwardness, refined her
performance of herself as a loveless wretch. Poor thing, we
think, briefly.

I need to sit.

*She sits. Tries three distinct ways of sitting in a chair. Thoughtful and
attentive, first. Relaxed and open, second. As simply and unexpressively
as a person can sit in chair, third.*

I need to stand.

She stands. Posed as if for soliloquy.

How to be, or, not, or, what, because, you try, and get hurt,

and wait in lines, you stand around humming, and for what
for, exactly? And do you want to change, or just leave?
Meaning what? Unknown. Except, more being scared, and
night sweats and day sweats and overthinking everything
and getting whiter all the time, and, didn't we used to be
so enterprising and fine, once, in the mud puddles with the
yellow rubber boots and our little bones and the trees and
everything so full of ribbons and daylight? Before the losses
piled up into a shape as big as we are? I have no idea. What a
life, I guess, what a goddamned life, ours. Very pretty, really,
if you have someone to talk about it with. I suppose. Don't
know. This is just one person's opinion.

Pause.

A butterfly in Massachusetts flaps its wings, and, a whale
dies, off the coast of Iceland. Meanwhile, in Argentina, a
man and woman, hand-not-in-hand, look for somewhere
to eat. Meanwhile, in another city, two people are on a
trampoline, laughing. Or someone is betting on a horse race.
Now the butterfly dies, the whale washes up somewhere.
No connection, or, none known. This is the world and Jen
is at school, rearranging herself in her chair, thinking about
herself, her life, everyone else. Her classmates, one by one,
come forward with some little something, some hastily
arranged half-sentences to describe it. A girl with old ice
skates, a boy with a comic book in French. Someone with his
brother, who is retarded, another with a photo of her mother
on a camel. Jen is thinking of words she can say.

Brief pause.

Such faces, yours, so tragic around the mouth. Yes, what a lot
of nice white people here tonight.

Note to self: Dear me. I don't know what you want from me.

Brief pause.

I broke my arm in a foreign country once. No language, the wrong money, couldn't describe the pain, so, no one could help. I was offered words without vowels, small portions of uncomforting food. I tried to be still, I shook. An animal at the veterinarians. As far away as you could get. I don't think that country's even still a country. And now I stand before you now. Believing things are different. Yelp. Bark. Growl. Yawn. Probably Not. Maybe.

Jennifer's teacher says, Jennifer?

Somewhere somewhere else, the blue shirt and sunglasses are clearing customs, nothing to declare, smiling or crying or neither, how would I know. Hard to know. When the person who speaks to your soul doesn't talk to you anymore. And there you are, left not knowing what to say, stripped of your previous meanings. Maybe you touch your hair. You don't know what to do. Leaving you like Jennifer, who moves to the front of the room.

And what have you brought in for us, today?, the teacher asks.

This, Jennifer says, holding nothing.

The children sit there, like you, and she takes off her black shoes. It was nice to be held, to not feel alone. She takes off her socks. The children, like you, say nothing. Like my weakling, the town crier, now departed. For my thing, I brought in this, she says, and takes off her dress, her underwear. She is naked before them. He said nice things, sometimes, when he spoke. I thought he was fewer people. This is my arms. This is from where I fell once. The teacher is slowly hyperventilating. These are my little feet, she says, pointing. This is for being a girl. I like running. A pet dog someone brought in barks. Hands slowly go up. Where did you get it, one boy asks. It's mine, she says. Can we touch it, a boy with asthma asks, breathing wrong. Jennifer stands still. He told me I was beautiful. I started thinking I was beautiful. Some of the children cried. I don't have anything. I have a house and some family and people I know and toys and I don't have anything. She stands there. I stand here. Naked and controlling the shaking. Trying to fall in love with breathing. Everyone looking and seeing. I've disappointed you, I can tell, my dress still on. Try to understand. I'm cold. She says. We were quite a pair. Back in the day. It's a big ocean, the Atlantic. Fuck it. To be loved and held. That's all, she says. Love. Keep high watch. Your time is coming. This is all that's left of me. This, she says. Look at lucky you. All so beautiful, so countable, and inconsolable. *(Brief pause.)* Have we lost anyone? *(She quickly scans the audience.)* Of course we have. And all stare straight ahead. As she puts on her clothes and stands there, clothed, hoping they saw her or understood, wanting everything to be different, or over. That's all. And what a lovely ending– all of us here, no longer waiting, the pretty light leaving all the pretty eyes. Look at you all. Ghost-white with life and your own terrible secret. Live with it and never tell anyone. Good night.

And now to bed. The End, yes?

Lights fade to black, as she begins to undress.

End.

MR THEATRE COMES HOME DIFFERENT

1998

DRAMATIS PERSONAE

MR THEATRE

Setting: *The stage set of a living room. A table with a telephone and a vase of flowers on it.*

MR THEATRE

He enters with an open umbrella. He shakes the rain off of it and places it in a stand. He checks his watch, takes his coat off, looks around as if expecting someone. He ponders over the set and, then, he sees the audience. He stares. He stands. He starts to leave and then turns around. He flips the table out of his way, kicks the chairs over.

Strike the set! Strike the world! My former life, gone!
Everything stricken, struck, gotten rid of. Now, set the stage
again for something nothing less than me: some man, a
wound; an animal, with English. Here I am. I am come! Born
from the wings, or somewhere in the back of the theatre.
Alone. *(He sees the telephone.)* But whom have we here?
Someone? *(He picks up the telephone.)* Hello? No one? Prop.
(He throws the telephone aside. He notices a flower on the floor.)
Speaking of nature– which I was, and still am, and always
will be– here is some that someone planted here. *(He picks it
up.)* Good evening, flower. Did you grow today? Get some
sun? Look at you, you lovely fresh cut dying thing. Have you
come to upstage me? *(He eats the flower.)* That tasted the way
you would think a flower should. *(He chews.)* This last, I find
a terribly suggestive remark. But I meant for it to suggest or
augur nothing; beyond that of my darker purpose, which is,
in fact, dark. Is, in deed, darker. But, between you, me and
the lighting, I should tell you, in an aside: whisper, whisper,
whisper.

Gentle's none, my name is blank. And I have come and
kicked things over. I have breathed badly. I will act quickly,
entertain myself, and then leave. This is my character, as I
would have you have it; and this, my interior life, as I would,
for you, outwardly live it. *(He kicks a chair off stage. Laughing.)*
But I– I would like you to know– I yearn.

Witness me yearn.

(On bended knee.) My love! my love! if you are out there: why don't you love me, and why aren't you out there? I should look up your old address. So as for us to enact the love scene that is coming. That is here. Now! Kiss my moving mouth. I am all afire, burning. *(He purses his lips as if to kiss, closes his eyes, and rises to stand on the tips of his toes. He stands, so, and then opens his eyes and unpurses his lips.)* By the way, the fire exits are located here and here, and in the event of a fire, or should you hear a fire alarm, or should you see someone run screaming past you in flames, or simply should you panic, anxious, and seek to suffer alone, like an injured thing does, please use the doors, either there or there, and peaceably remove yourself. But not now, stay seated now, for the climax– if I can make it come– is coming. Something climactic is nigh.

Here cometh the storm scene! Shaken by a teenage stagehand from a box up in the flies! Rise! Rain your fake rain and drown the fake world! Make the paint peel and the floorboards buckle! Come sideways, hail, sleet, serious weather, rain! Ruin every wedding and parade! Mess up my hair, make my bones ache! Wrack, weather! Wrack!

But first, stop.

Not so fast.

Here comes the calm. The calm during the storm. Do you hear birds singing? I don't. And it's for me that they're not singing. No explanation is needed. But as for exposition: you should see certain parts of my anatomy. You should see the mess of bed I rise from in the afternoon, looking in a mirror to see the damage done in the night, checking myself for some rare infection and or new sore having come. Making sure– ensuring– that my hair and gums and face are all receding, leaving me left with only eyes left left to stare from. And I stare. Hands in lap, I think of one Easter, one spring;

me in a suit, clean; the world sparkling; hunting scenes on the
dishes; the feet beneath the table. But enough talk of mirrors
and of reflections of what once was but now is no longer.

Where were we? I believe, over here. And in love, wasn't it?
It was sweet, wasn't it? But now it's over, is it not? When I'm
gone, I'll be gone. I wish the little life I lived tonight were
different. Were more lived. But I am glad I ate that flower.
Would that the world entire were a flower for me to eat.
And would that my faked feelings could make Yours Truly
genuine. But the death scene! I almost forgot. Not surprising.
But, here, now: the end, at last.

Pretend I am dying. *(He begins to die. He drops to a knee.)*
Pretend my life was wasted. *(He dies more.)* That I spent my
time in this body on this earth dumbly. *(He stops.)* Pretend
you loved me. *(He stands.)* I smell bad, and I am in a hospital.
I am your mother. *(He carries the table off-stage. Throughout the
remainder of this paragraph he is striking the set.)* Pretend I am
your mother; that you loved me when little, that then you
then stopped for some time, but have started up again, in
time for me to die. Pretend it's hard to look. My eyes and
breasts, nothing on my body looks the way it's supposed
to look. You mother me. You stand there, pretend, and you
mother your mother, who is dying. Or I'm your child, and I
cannot breathe, as you stand above me, breathing. Or, I am–
pretend– you. Whoever– I am dying. Pretend this: that this is
not pretend. Pretend you are sitting there. And that this was
good. Pretend I'm crying. That you're crying. And that this is
the end. I start to go. I don't look at you. It seems familiar. It
seems resolved. *(He picks up his umbrella, holds it as if a cane.)*
Pretend that this is over. That it will not go on, interminably,
The End. People coming and going. Entering and exiting.
Forever. *(He comes downstage.)*

Give yourselves a big hand.

You were lovely.

I die.

Snow starts to fall. We are in rapture. A bloodhound crouches near, there, by a freezing river, in a darkening wood. And your hands are cold. And our happy world is ended. Pretend.

He shakes umbrella, repeats opening gestures, as lights fade.

End.

9 781559 369596